‖‖‖ ‖ ‖ ‖‖‖‖‖‖ ‖ ‖‖‖‖ ‖‖‖‖ ‖‖‖‖‖‖‖ ‖‖ ‖‖

The ZOLA Experience

KATURAH A BRYANT, MS-LMFT, BSN-RN, LADC

Founder and Creator of "THE ZOLA EXPERIENCE"
A Certificate Program for Providers

Copyright © GAG 2020 ALL DOMESTIC AND INTERNATIONAL RIGHTS RESERVED, NO LAWFUL COPY OF THIS MATERIAL IS PERMITTED WITHOUT PERMISSION OF THE AUTHOR.

ISBN: 9798670866408

PIMOSH Publishing Company (USA)
P.O. BOX 7077 - Matthews NC, 28105
Toll Free: 844.4.PIMOSH (746674)

DEDICATION

This book is dedicated to everyone who has ever longed and loved for someone, or something that is no more.

CONTENTS

ACKNOWLEDGMENTS

First and foremost, I want to give thanks and praise to the Creator.

Writing a "book" has always been something I talked about doing. I thought it'd be an autobiographical document. I began my writing journey in graduate school as an outlet for the stress of going to school full time, experiencing a public divorce, parenting three teenagers and working full time. Writing and journaling were great outlets, and it has been something that I've continued throughout the years.

Life got in my way, and my focus shifted. I never stopped writing, and I was encouraged along the way by friends who saw "something in me" that needed to be put on paper and shared with the world. One thing I've learned to embrace on this journey is to listen to my intuitive voice and to hold on to my dreams. In divine time your heart's desires come to pass.

I was led by Spirit to develop The ZOLA Experience. God laid it out for me to have four years of working out the curriculum; I'm grateful for that. The concept laid dormant for four years after that time. In the midst of the COVID-19 pandemic and fueled by social unrest, God spoke to me again and that voice said it was time to give attention to The ZOLA Experience again.

And so I embarked on the journey to offer this brief, seven-session treatment intervention to the world. The world is in such need of love and healing today. Healers and treaters are always looking for a tool to help support clients on their healing journey, especially recovery from loss. We often don't have a simple tool to aide and enhance our practice in this area. The ZOLA Experience answers that need.

In addition to God, thank you to my Ancestors, Angels and Guides. I thank my children, Aquil, Hafeeza and Nadir, for the many talents and skills they have been blessed with and the life lessons we have shared on this life journey.

Dolores "Dee Brown," my mentor, teacher, spiritual sister, and Angel Guide. Dr. Lonnie Garris, Jr., for his loving support. Jamilah Munir for agreeing to edit my work with her sisterly eye. Ellen Boynton for her sisterly love and wisdom. My brother, Guy, for his encouragement.

I'm grateful for my sister, Regina B. Fields, for being the legal eagle that she is. I thank my "Super Bowl Crew" who supported me along the way, giving me insight, laughter and love. Your positive energy is so greatly appreciated. To every client who honored me by allowing me to guide them on their journey of recovery, thank you. You gave me a testing ground for my divinely inspired ideas.

A special thank you to H. K. Hill Funeral Services family, Khalfani Radio and Global Alchemy Group for giving me a platform to share The ZOLA Experience with the world. To the ZOLA Team who trusted and believed in me, your professionalism and feedback was invaluable. As the recording artist, song writer and my "brother," Victor Fields of Regina Records wrote, "Open your heart. Love lives inside of you." This is the essence of The ZOLA Experience.

Peace.
Katurah A. Bryant

KATURAH A. BRYANT BIO

Katurah A. Bryant, MS-LMFT, BSN-RN, LADC, is the Founder of The ZOLA Experience: A Journey of Recovery From Loss. The ZOLA Experience is a simple proven tool for providers to help move clients through grief and loss. As the CEO of Global Alchemy Group, she heads the Training Division. This Division specializes in Cultural Competence training in health care delivery, supervision, health and wellness retreats and staff development.

Ms. Bryant is a Licensed Marriage Family Therapist, Registered Nurse, Licensed Alcohol and Drug Counselor and a Certified Clinical Supervisor. During her 36-year career, she has held many notable leadership positions, including:

- Assistant Clinical Director at the Connecticut Mental Health Center, Substance Abuse Treatment Unit, New Haven, CT

- Nurse/Research Therapist at Yale University, New Haven, CT

- Consultant to various agencies in Connecticut, New Jersey and New York

- Private practice clinician

Katurah is passionate about her work. Her motto is, "If I can add value to one person's life today, it will be a blessed day".

Katurah enjoys dancing (line dancing and swing-out swing dancing), power walks, and is a Life Member of Alpha Kappa Alpha Sorority, Inc.

THE ZOLA EXPERIENCE

The
Zen peacefulness when
One is open to
Love
Again

THE ZOLA EXPERIENCE
A JOURNEY OF RECOVERY FROM LOSS

Love is.....
by Lonnie Garris, Jr.

Love has every man's definition.
To some it is the highest form of human
feeling,
      radiation and resonance.

(To me) Love is simplicity .
It is the glow in the ashes when the flames
have finally diminished.
It is what's left when the excitement is gone.

Love is strong but simple.
Love is firm but tender.
Love is simply caring.

      This is The ZOLA Experience

THE ZOLA EXPERIENCE
A JOURNEY OF RECOVERY FROM LOSS

KATURAH A BRYANT
MS-LMFT, BSN-RN, LADC

Founder and Creator of The ZOLA Experience

A Certificate Program For Providers

The Purposeful Struggle

One morning in the middle of morning meditation and affirmations, I began thinking about the grandness of The Creator. The Creator is always purposeful. There is nothing in existence that does not have purpose. Everything has impact on the global and universal balance of things. The Creator created everything to be interdependent in order to maintain balance and to remind us that the least of things is as important as the greatest of things.

I love butterflies. Butterflies are light, beautiful, resilient and truly a symbol of change at its essence. The journey of the butterfly is truly a miracle. Each stage is a divine miracle of purpose, starting with a larvae/egg placed gently on a leaf. For some butterfly species, it has to be a specific leaf to support their life. From that egg comes the caterpillar, the second stage of the development of the butterfly.

The sole purpose of the caterpillar is to prepare for the next phase of development, the cocoon phase. To prepare for the cocooning, the caterpillar may consume leaves to 40 times its original weight. When its purpose is complete, it finds just the right branch to settle upon to spin its silk cocoon.

The real magic happens during the chrysalis phase. The body of the caterpillar almost totally liquifies, leaving purposeful cells to develop the mature butterfly. In divine time the butterfly matures and works its way out of the cocoon with purposeful struggle. It is through this struggle that the wings get pumped with blood. When the butterfly emerges, it is able to take wing and fly. Butterflies are also pollinators and impact the food chain. Their other purpose is to add beauty and joy as they flit in and about our lives.

Bees are another example of the Creator's design for interdependency within the cycle of change. We humans, at least prior to the COVID-19 shut down, were profit driven and spewing toxic, bee-killing chemicals on vegetation. The toxic environment was not allowing the bees to actualize their "purpose" as part of the ecosystem. As a result, the global food supply was impacted. Their purpose of pollinating vegetables, flowers, fruit and trees was stifled. Just one element "off," in the delicate balance of nature, adversely impacted our very existence.

We received instruction from the Infinite Spirit on how to reverse the negative impact on our environment: Honor the Creator and the Creation.

Another example of seemingly small things having a big impact is the COVID-19 virus. We humans have co-existed with viruses and bacteria since the beginning of time, and COVID-19, with its different strains, is only one of them. There are thousands of viruses and bacteria in our system naturally. When you have too much of a virus, you become imbalanced, sick, "dis-eased." Just one element, a microscopic germ, can throw off the delicate balance of our health as human beings and threaten our very existence.

When we talk about spiritual balance, the Creator's word is simple too. In all major spiritual thought, to maintain our spiritual balance, we only need to do two things.

1. Honor the Creator/God Consciousness with every fiber of one's being.
2. Honor our fellow human being, recognizing that every human being is the image of God.

The Creator is never without purpose. The ultimate core of every thing is the essence of the Creator, Love. We are all in the midst of our own ZOLA Experience journey. If we take the time to reflect on the pure essence of the Creator in all we do, we will recognize the essence of The ZOLA Experience, which is LOVE.

If one truly embraces the greeting "Namaste," which means the God (consciousness) in me honors the God in you, all of our social ills would be eliminated.

The Bible describes this God consciousness by defining "love" in I Corinthians 13:1-13. The writer notes in the last sentence of the last verse, "But the Greatest of these is LOVE." Of all of creation, humans are the only living thing that is given "free will." As human beings we are given free will to serve and submit to the Creator as an act of gratitude for God's beneficence, mercy and love. By submitting to the essence of the Creator we experience Love. Our purpose therefore is to be about Love. When we talk about finding one's purpose, finding one's passion, and the beauty of living a purposely driven life, the pontification is reflective of The ZOLA Experience. It is about living a life journey of Love.

Love heals all things. Love is the essence of joy in all things. Love is the purpose of all things. A common statement describing when one finds their purpose is that they love what they are doing and would do it even if they were not paid. One would ask, Why? Because the Spiritual rewards manifest in abundance beyond measure. It is when you walk in the God consciousness that you journey in The ZOLA Experience, a journey of love and recovery from life's challenges.

THE ZOLA EXPERIENCE
A JOURNEY OF RECOVERY FROM LOSS

INTRODUCTION

There are some absolutes in this life; *change* is one of them. *death* is the other. We will all transition to a higher vibration. We will all "die" and physically leave the shell of our bodies. We all will change, either by the passing of time, or, willfully toward self-actualization, wholeness of self. My dear friend and mentor says:

"Give Time time. All things will change."

Brown, MS-MFT, LADC

The quote is a metaphor for addressing any challenge that confronts us. All of us have attempted to change major things in our lives. Many have been successful. Challenges are inclusive of the desire to have a more balanced lifestyle, to make healthier dietary choices, to exercise, spiritual challenges (i.e. addictions and recovery); mental health (e.g. family of origin issues or intimate relationships), and the desire to be a more authentic human being.

Each challenge is a journey to self. As with most journeys, it takes effort to change and to reach a stated destination. We must think of life as such a journey, with many stops, starts, turns and challenges along the way. One thing is certain, change, like all journeys, begins with the first step.

I was blessed to develop The ZOLA Experience curriculum for a brief grief and loss intervention. The program was initially introduced at the Howard K. Hill Funeral Services (HKHFS) in New Haven, Connecticut. Providing support to help families heal after a loss is an idea I've held for quite some time. My research shows that the funeral industry does very little for families, post funeral. Many offer "online resources." Some refer families to local faith-based organizations that offer some pastoral grief counseling.

I listened to my intuitive voice. My spirit moved me to approach Mr. Howard K. Hill after the funeral services of a friend that HKHFS serviced. He agreed to meet with me to explore such an idea. I appreciate Mr. Hill for being open and forward thinking enough to allow me to offer this unique experience to the HKHFS families.

Initially, the curriculum focused on the loss of a loved one and was de-signed for a group setting. However, in private practice this intervention is found to be equally impactful in an individual setting. You can use this intervention to support people being confronted with loss from a myriad of things, not just that of a transitioned loved one. For this reason, I will use the following generic term, "lost love object," throughout to describe the object of the loss.

"Grieving is what enables you to go forward after a loss. It helps you so that you can give love again."

R. Remen
The Little Book of Kitchen Table Wisdom

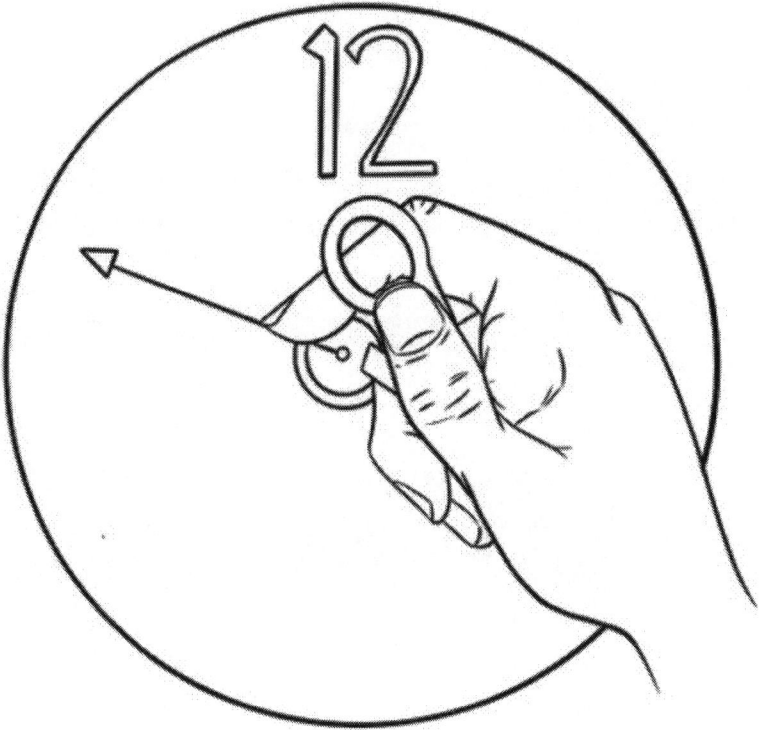

"We all will change, either by the passing of time, or, willfully toward self-actualization, wholeness of self"

~ Katurah

WELCOME TO THE ZOLA EXPERIENCE

Grieving from a loss is as unique to the individual as one's fingerprints. No two people go through this process alike. The commonality of the experience of grief after a loss is that we all will experience it, and we all must find our way through the experience.

Recovering from loss is a "process," not an event. When we think about our lives over the spectrum of time, we see that we have experienced and overcome the intense feelings that come with loss. We see too that we have been able to go on with our lives. As the Elders say, "Just live long enough." We possess everything we need to get through the experience of loss and the life lessons that come with it.

Sometimes one must dig deep to find understanding from a loss. There are other times when the loss is clearly a mental and physical relief for the one who has transitioned as well as those that remain on this side of the plane. Regardless, the Universe makes no mistakes, and it becomes our job to understand the wisdom in the actions of one's Higher Power.

The ZOLA Experience is the essence of the process of grief, as well as the essence of life. "Zola" is a word of African origin that means "to love." Moving past the intensity of loss, not becoming or remaining "stuck," is a true testament of Love...love of self as well as love of the lost love object that is no longer there.

It is always an honor to journey with clients and families who take the risk to embrace The ZOLA Experience. It is important that you, the facilitator, recognize the courage it takes to work through the thoughts and feelings after one has experienced a loss.

The client may continue to struggle, but at this moment in time, they choose to take a risk and give themselves permission to begin their healing process. We also recognize that it is truly about LOVE.

Brene` Brown, in her book, The Gifts of Imperfection, writes about the value of vulnerability and love in our quest of "wholehearted living." She states that you cannot separate the two. In the midst of struggles, losses and/or challenges, the thing that wholehearted individuals have in common is they develop practices that enable them to hold on to the belief that they are worthy of belonging, worthy of joy and even worthy of love.

This too, is the essence of The ZOLA Experience. To support the client in developing a practice that enables them to embrace, once again, the belief that they are worthy of belonging, to experience joy in their life and most importantly, to believe they are worthy to love again.

The ZOLA Experience is designed as a brief intervention, seven (7) sessions. The sessions are most impactful in a group setting. However, the sessions can be facilitated in an individual setting with minimal modifications.

Whenever you bring folks together, each one carries their own energy into the experience. The group will come together creating an identity uniquely theirs.

The seven (7) sessions of The ZOLA Experience are designed to be facilitated by experienced individual and/or group facilitators to support members on their journey to love. Depending on the group size and make up, it is important that there are two facilitators, as there is a module that focuses specifically on gender identity regarding self-care and the recovery process.

The suggested length of in-person group sessions is two hours: 30 minutes for members to arrive early if there is a need to meet with the clinician prior to the group session; 60 minute group session; 30 minutes at the end of the session in the event further "closure" is needed or a referral is necessary.

Virtual meetings can be set up and those having questions can be accommodated outside of the session at a mutually agreed upon time.

> **"Love is the medicine that accelerates the process of healing"**
>
> M. Ruiz
> **The Mastery of Love**

THE ZOLA EXPERIENCE
A JOURNEY OF RECOVERY FROM LOSS

GETTING TO KNOW YOU

THE ZOLA EXPERIENCE

Introduction to Session no. 1
Building a Foundation of Support

I was looking for "THE" logo to express the vision of The ZOLA Experience. I was finding it a challenge trying to find it. The "I" was the problem as I recognize that The ZOLA Experience is about building a community of support on this journey of recovery from loss.

I humbled myself and "asked" the Universe to "bring the right logo" to me that would speak to the essence of this experience. Some may express this as "I prayed over it." "Ask and it shall be given." I asked and it was given to me, fluttering in my thoughts much like the butterfly.

When I saw the butterfly gently settled in the hands, it said so much. I saw the delicate resilience of the butterfly in its colorful black and white beauty. Understanding the remarkable metamorphosis of the butterfly, I also recognize recovery from loss is no less a miracle.

The hands symbolized the support one needs in their recovery process, as the palms create a safe space for a soft landing in this challenging world we live in. The palms are open to allow the butterfly to take flight into the world.

The 10 fingers are those things that support your journey of recovery and help you stay grounded and in the moment, i.e. friends/family you can call 24/7, faith based community support, a mantra or a prayer, a favorite place inside and/or outside of the home that is calming and brings a sense of peace, like the beach or somewhere in nature, or perhaps your ZOLA Experience "family."

Yellow is a happy color. Yellow symbolizes the healing power of the sun and the hope that a new day brings.

Your willingness to participate in The ZOLA Experience speaks to your openness for change and the possibility to love life again. We will join together on this journey of recovery from loss.

SESSION NO. 1:

Getting to Know You "Questions"
Joining as a Group

Materials: Blank papers to note time line; tape; journals; pens; folders; reflective reading material (e.g. book excerpts, printed copy, affirmations, cards, etc.)

Exercise: Using the Locogram

The primary focus of the first session is for the group to join and begin the process of coalescing. Also, participants are allowed to see each other as a resource to move past current feelings of grief and loss.

The primary focus of the individual session is for the client to identify areas where they have overcome challenges in their life. Additionally, it allows them to identify the resources that supported them and enabled them to move on in their lives.

For the group or the individual session, the goal is for the members to   validate their strengths and abilities to overcome "loss" and to move on past the intense pain.

Beginning each session with the reflective reading aides in the joining process. It brings the group, and the individual, "into the room" and allows participants to settle before beginning the exercise.

THE LOCOGRAM EXERCISE:

The purpose of this joining exercise has many layers that can be explored. Initially it begins by building trust between the members and the facilitators.

The facilitators use paper to make a timeline in the room. Each group member volunteers to note the year of the earliest recollection of a significant loss and the most recent experience of a lost love object. The facilitator uses tape to mark off the spaces where each member places themselves along the timeline.

The timeline covers the span of time for members to reflect on their historical journey of loss and recovery. The timeline can be marked in decades, years or months, depending on the group make up.

There are a number of questions posed to the group as the members move to the different spaces on the timeline:

- When was your **first recollection** of a lost love object that was significant in your life?

- When was the **most recent recollection** of a lost love object that was significant in your life?

- From the first to the most recent recollection, have members of the group position themselves on the timeline where they "feel" they belong. (It should be noted that an individual can move between two positions on the timeline, in the case of a distant loss and a recent loss for example.)

The facilitator then asks members at each position on the timeline to share with the group.

Some examples of questions might be:

- Who in the group is experiencing daily challenges dealing with the recovery from the loss? Who in the group had an experience like that in the past? What insight can they share about getting past the daily challenge(s)?

- Those at recent loss, what would they like to ask those with more distant losses?

- Those with distant losses, what would they like to say to those with recent losses?

- Those with middle positions on the timeline, what would they like to say to those with distant losses as well as those with recent losses?

The purpose of this exercise is to validate for the participants that they have the tools to recover from the pain of loss. There's history that validates this as well and is highlighted by the resources in the room. We know that recovery is possible and is a process unique to the individual. The group members become aware that they are capable of moving on with their lives, while holding onto the lost love object.

This is also a time for the facilitators to point out the rich resources in the group to support each other in the healing process.

For the Individual client, their strengths are validated, and they are supported as well.

At the conclusion of the session, the facilitators will hand out the journals, folders and pens and the journal writing exercise session no. 2: "How is Your Spiritual Walk Impacting Your Recovery From Your Loss?"

Members are encouraged to use the journal to write down their thoughts and feelings over the next seven (7) sessions, in addition to assigned writing exercises.

Journaling is a great projective exercise that oftentimes fosters a release of feelings as well as an opportunity to gain insight about self and the situation.

"Love stretches your heart and makes you big inside"

M. Walker

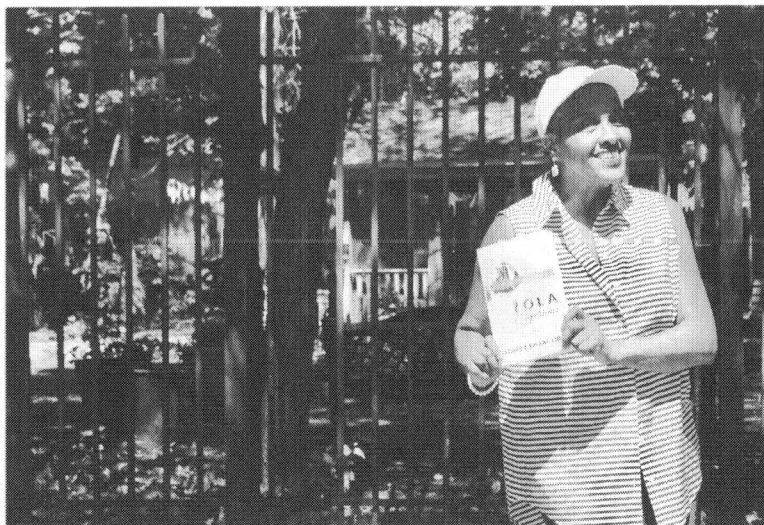

HANDOUT FOR SESSION NO. 2
JOURNALING TOPIC:

How is Your Spiritual Walk Impacting Your Recovery From Your loss?

"Love is the language in which God speaks and when we listen with love, it is the heart that hears"

Healing Runes, Love

THE ZOLA EXPERIENCE
A JOURNEY OF RECOVERY FROM LOSS

KATURAH A BRYANT.
MS-LMFT. BSN-RN, LADC
KATURAH@GLOBALACHEMYGROUP.COM

"It is when you walk in the GOD consciousness that you journey in The ZOLA Experience"

~ Katurah

FAITHFILLED FEELINGS
THE ZOLA EXPERIENCE

Introduction to Session no. 2
We've Come This Far By Faith

Building a Foundation of Support

As a clinician I often marveled at the metamorphosis of clients as they embraced the process of recovery. I love this about the work I continue to have passion for.

Clients would come to treatment broken and defeated by their life circumstances and choices. Choices result in multiple losses for some. Loss of health, loss of family, loss of healthy support, loss of spiritual health, loss of self to the control of external forces like the judicial system, child protective services and addiction.

This "loss" would often be expressed in aggressive behavior or depression and a myriad of behaviors in-between.

The primary challenge was to rebuild, and in some cases build, self esteem to support clients on their journey to love of self. If you are depleted of love of self, you have no energy to give to others or things that may be important for a quality life.

I honored the fact of the courage clients possessed to cross the threshold and enter a world that for many had not been kind or understanding of their life's journey. I acknowledged the daunting and overwhelming "systems" putting demands on their behavior as they were functioning from a place layered in losses.

I would validate for them the unspoken that brought on the aggression or the silence of the depression. I recognized for them that there was no reason for them to trust me in supporting them on their journey of recovery from loss.

Trust was something that I was willing to earn from them. I assured them that I would "carry the hope of recovery" for them until they could carry it for themselves, empowering them to know they were in charge of how their recovery would manifest.

For me, it is an act of love.

"It is when you walk in the God consciousness that you journey in The ZOLA Experience, a journey of love and recovery from life's challenges"

Katurah

SESSION NO. 2:
"We've Come This Far by Faith"

Spirituality in the Face of Loss and Grief

At the beginning of the session, the facilitators check in with the group. The use of a reflective reading can be used at this time each week as well. Encourage reflections and insights from the previous session.

Materials: journal; handout for session no. 2.

"How is Your Spiritual Walk Impacting Your Recovery From Your Loss?"

Exercise: Share journal writing reflecting on the session no. 2 handout.

This session is often challenging for the group as well as the individual. Given their history and/or the nature of the loss, seeking comfort and balance with a "Higher Power" is often a challenge. Clients may be experiencing a myriad of thoughts and feelings such as anger, shame, guilt, or abandonment associated with the loss and their relationship with their "Higher Power."

Facilitators support the group to explore such issues as:

- The difference between spirituality and religion
- The messages from their family of origin about spirituality and/or religion
- Client's relationship with a "Higher Power," historically; how they express this relationship; how this relationship has served them throughout life

Group members are encouraged and supported to read their response to the writing assignment. The facilitators will support the group to process thoughts and feelings associated with their reflection. This is also the process for working with the individual client. Upon the conclusion of the session, facilitators will hand out the journal writing exercise for session no. 3.

Reflection Exercise:
Messages from Family of Origin/Self Care

> *"Children learn what they live....*
> *Adults live what they've learned*
> - Katurah

HANDOUT FOR SESSION NO. 3
JOURNALING TOPIC:

"Adults Live What They've Learned"

Complete the reflection exercise:
Messages from Family of Origin/Self-Care

As you write in your journal reflect on the following questions:

1. What was your first experience with a significant loss, i.e. family member through death, divorce, geographical distance, incarceration, illness, loss of a pet, etc.?
   - How old were you?
   - How did you feel?

2. How did your family/close friends handle it?
   - Did they talk about it?
   - Did they have any "ceremonies"/ rituals?
   - Did you grieve openly as a family?
   - What role did spirituality/religion play in this process?
   - What was your reaction?
     - Was your reaction

- encouraged/tolerated?
- suppressed/shut down?

3. What kind of messages about loss/dying/ grieving were you left with from this and other early loss experiences?
   - Good grief and closure?
   - Puzzlement, questions?
   - Resentment for not being included?
   - Unresolved grief?

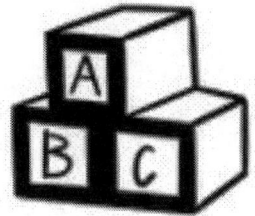

"Children learn what they live

Adults live what they've learned"

~ Katurah

ADULT LEARNERS
THE ZOLA EXPERIENCE

Introduction to Session no. 3
"ADULTS LIVE WHAT THEY'VE LEARNED"

Dorthy Law Nolte, PhD, whose popular poster is displayed on my office wall, says: *Children Learn What They Live*. I would take it a step further and state that adults live what they've learned.

The poster lists a number of behaviors and traits that children would take on if they experienced certain things over a period of time. For example, if a child lives with criticisms, they learn to condemn. If a child lives with praise, they learn to appreciate. If a child lives with acceptance, they learn to love.

These are "messages" from one's family of origin or the family you grew up with. The "code" of behavior is learned and normalized by the family system. These messages influence behavior, both healthy and unhealthy, far beyond childhood.

Some behaviors become a cultural norm. The message and example of how the family and community deal with loss is one of those situations that takes on a cultural norm. Self care is another concept that reflects the cultural norm of the family and community.

One begins to challenge their "norm" once you become an adult and discover that your "normal behavior" no longer serves you in a productive way. At that moment, one may contemplate changing the message and the behavior.

People change because they become uncomfortable, and insight has little to do with change. At that moment of discomfort, one is faced with two options, either repair or repeat. Repair is the unknown of choosing to do things differently and pushing through feelings of discomfort to get to a healthier desired place. Repeat is what I describe as choosing to stay in one's "negative comfort zone." It's negative in the context that there is an awareness that the **choices** being made are not healthy.

It's a "comfort zone" because it's familiar— the "what I always do" even though there's an awareness that it is not a healthy space to be in and the outcome is predictable, even known, and undesirable.

The blessing of being an "adult" is that you can change the tape when the message no longer serves you in a way that allows you to move forward in you life.

The Serenity Prayer speaks to adults about acceptance and change, advising us to "to accept the things I cannot change."

If embracing acceptance as a child is the foundation of love, acceptance of loss is an important piece of the foundation of the journey of recovery from loss. The culmination of one's journey to discover love, of self and love of the lost love object, is the essence of The ZOLA Experience.

"Mostly people change not because they see the light but because they feel the heat."

Anonymous

IN-SESSION HANDOUTS FOR SESSION NO. 3

DON'T LET STRESS MANAGE YOU!!!
TIPS TO HELP YOU MANAGE YOUR STRESS...
Katurah A. Bryant, MS-LMFT, BSN-RN, LADC

❖ IDENTIFY YOUR TRIGGERS
- o What are some of the sources of your stress
- o Identify patterns
- o Make a conscious effort to CHANGE your "pattern" or response to the situation

"THE ONLY PERSON YOU CAN CHANGE OR HAVE CONTROL OF IS... SELF"!!

❖ PRACTICE DAILY MEDITATION/PRAYER
  ○ The goal: to QUIET THE MIND…to get centered
  ○ To enter a relaxed state
  ○ Focus on a mantra or image

"THE GOAL IS TO CLEAR THE MIND AND LET GO OF STRESS!!

@GAG 2020 ALL RIGHTS RESERVED. NO LAWFUL COPYING OF THIS MATERIAL IS PERMITTED WITHOUT PERMISSION OF THE AUTHOR.

❖ SUGGESTIONS ON HOW TO "DE-STRESS"

➢ MASSAGE
  ○ Shown to relieve stress and improve mood

➢ AROMATHERAPY
  ○ Calming affect
  ○ Citrus, Rose, Sage and Lavender scents have been found to be effective stress relievers

➢ ACUPUNCTURE
  ○ Acupuncture-NADA Protocol is a group experience known to aid in stress management and foster a sense of relaxation

➢ BREATHING EXERCISES
  ○ To give your mind and body a "quick time out"
  ○ Can be used anywhere, at any time

PRACTICE THIS BREATHING EXERCISE:

- ○ Ground yourself: place feet flat on floor; hands on thighs
- ○ Close your eyes (if you feel safe)
- ○ Take a slow deep breath through your nose and exhale through pursed lips to the count of eight (8)
- ○ Envision yourself breathing in the "calm" and exhaling the "stress"
- ○ Repeat three (3) times
- ○ Do this simple stress reliever several times throughout your day for a "quick stress relief"
- ○ This exercise has been found to improve concentration and foster clarity of thought

➤ AEROBIC EXERCISES

- ○ Reduces anxiety and depression by stimulating the release of the "feel good" chemicals in the brain
- ○ Walking is the best exercise; it is low impact, inexpensive and can be done anywhere! The American Heart Association recommends 10K steps/ day...Remember, EVERY BIT COUNTS...
- ○ Take the stairs vs. the elevator
- ○ Park the car further from the door
- ○ Get off at an earlier bus or subway stop and walk the extra blocks
- ○ Join your children in a game of "tag" when you take them to the park
- ○ Start or join a "walking circle" to support each other to walk the recommended 20-30 minutes, 3-5 times per week

❖ DEVELOP A POSITIVE SUPPORT NETWORK
- o Spend time with positive friends and family
- o Care for a pet
- o Volunteer to help others
- o Join Al-anon; NAMI or other family support group
- o Become a member of a Faith Based Community

❖ TAPPING for Management of Stress (see instructional handout)
- o www.thetappingsolution.com

"I sustain myself with the love of family"
M. Angelou

Nick Ortner: Instructions for TAPPING to Manage Stress and Negative Thoughts
(Transcribed by K. Bryant, MS-LMFT, BSN-RN, LADC)

Nick Ortner: "Start with the negative side of the problem. **"If you are to clean the house you must see the dirt."**

Why you start with recognizing the stress. "I feel____"

THE ZOLA EXPERIENCE
A JOURNEY OF RECOVERY FROM LOSS

USING YOUR THREE MIDDLE FINGERS:

1. Side of hand crate chop either hand:
   - Say out loud: Even though I have all this ___ (anxiety; Stress; nervousness; sadness; anger) I choose to relax now; Repeat: even though I have... (name the feeling) All is well; I choose to relax and feel safe now

2. Eyebrow: tap gently; tune in to the stress

3. Side of eye; breathe gently

4. Under eyes: What am I so ...... about?

5. Under nose (between nose and top lip)

6. Under mouth: crease under the lip; acknowledge feelings: I'm feeling (identify the feeling)

7. Collar bone: Make a fist and tap (at the juncture in the middle of the chest); tune into the anxiety; begin to let go

8. Underneath the arm pit: tap gently while breathing gently

9. Top of head: tap and breathe gently

10. Assess awareness; then repeat until you feel relief

THE ZOLA EXPERIENCE
A JOURNEY OF RECOVERY FROM LOSS

Session 3

"Adults Live What They've Learned"

Messages from Family Of Origin/Self Care: Traditional and non-traditional avenues. It's all okay.

At the beginning of the session, the facilitators check in with the group. The use of a reflective reading can be used at this time each week as well. Encourage reflections and insights from the previous session.

Materials: Journal, Self-Care handouts and Breathing exercise.

Break out space: Self-care will be explored during this session. If it is a homogeneous group, a break out space may or may not be necessary depending on the size of the group.

Gender identification may be a consideration for this group, to foster open communication regarding "self-care". With the two facilitators it is best to do this exercise in a small group setting.

Exercise: Reflection of session no. 3 handout

This is an opportunity to explore messages from the family of origin and how grief and loss was expressed, as well as messages about self-care.

Facilitators can use the questions from the writing handout to support dialogue and exploration of thoughts and feelings. The challenge of this session is the focus on old family patterns and messages that are brought to the forefront.

In the breakout session facilitators will support clients to explore self-care and some of the suggested interventions. The additional handouts focus on suggestions for self-care, including a breathing exercise. It is important to emphasize the value of breath work.

Also, it is important for facilitators to explore and assess when to refer clients to seek professional mental health care to support the recovery process.

With about 20 minutes remaining, the breakout groups reconvene to the large group. Members reflect on the self-care suggestions.

The group practices some of the following interventions which they can do and share with their families/support network as stress relief:

- The breathing exercises
- Introduction to TAPPING (see handout on TAPPING)
- Introduction to Qigong (see NADA serenity prayer Qigong)
- Meditative walking (Hand out on meditative walking-Daily OM)
- Healing vibration of music (Handout on healing power of music)
- Aromatherapy: Be careful as many people have scent sensitivities. (Handout on Aromatherapy)
- Binaural Beats (YouTube)

Upon the conclusion of the session, the facilitators will hand out the journal exercise for session no.4: "An Open Letter to my Lost Loved Object".

Again, this can be modified to be whatever the "loss" is for the individual.

This is a timed exercise. The member is instructed to write in their journal using the hand-out as a guide for **15 minutes. No more, no less.** Be very clear about the time boundary. No edits. This is not going to be "graded'. Just free associate as the thoughts come.

Research notes there are brain changes when one puts pen to paper verses typing on a computer

HANDOUT FOR <u>SESSION NO. 4</u> <u>JOURNALING TOPIC:</u>

"The Benefits of Closure"
"An Open Letter to my Lost Love Object"

Imagine your lost love object were sitting in front of you:

1. What would you want to say?
2. What would they say to you?
3. What soul lesson was your lost love object teaching you?
4. What would your lost love object want you to do with your life NOW?

Instructions for this exercise:

Put pen to paper and begin to write whatever comes to mind for 15 minutes. Please set the timer and **<u>DO NOT GO OVER THE TIME LIMIT!! DO NOT WORRY ABOUT SPELLING OR GRAMMAR.</u>** Just allow your thoughts to flow on to the paper.

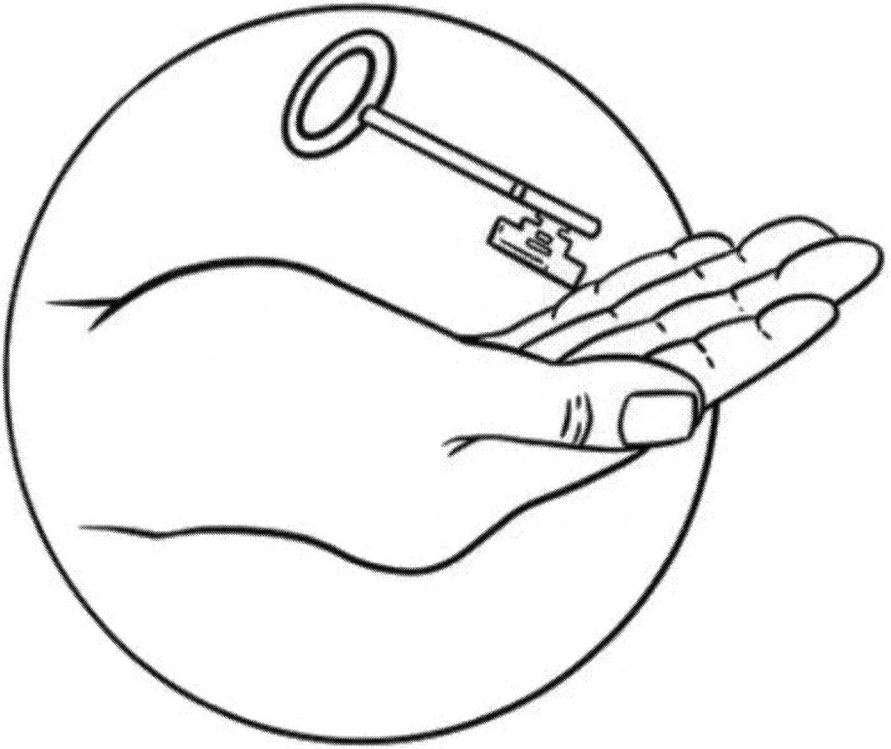

"There's comfort in knowing one is not alone in their struggle. Nothing is permanent inclusive of intense pain from loss"

~ Katurah

CLOSING CLOSETS

THE ZOLA EXPERIENCE

Introduction to Session no. 4
"The Benefits of Closure"
An Open Letter to my Lost Love Object

A loss is rarely perceived initially as being a good thing, a "blessing", or being "right on time". Loss generally leaves us with a sense of unanswered questions, or unspoken thoughts and feelings creating a void. We often hold on to this sense of a lack of closure surrounding the loss that can make one feel "stuck" and unable to move forward in their life.

In this age of "unorthodox loss" as a result of the global pandemic, this leads to another layer to experiencing loss and trying to seek closure. Loved ones are transitioning in isolation, and the caring family is left to resolve the loss via a "face time" event.

The ritual of death looks different for many cultures. The commonality is that there is a process. When this process is interrupted, closure becomes even more of a challenge.

People are becoming unemployed, with no real pathway to closure by finding other employment or source of income. As a result people are experiencing housing insecurity and some finding themselves homeless for the first time.

In these examples the common avenues of coping have been taken away. Many people are living in isolation. So who does one lean on for support, especially given that your support network may be experiencing the same.

One can ruminate for years on the "shoulda, woulda, coulda" of the event. Taking the time to freely and non-judgmentally express one's self about the lost love object is an important piece on one's journey of recovery from loss.

Session 4

> **"Every time you forgive, the universe changes"**
>
> W. Young, The Shack

At the beginning of the session, the facilitators check in with the group. The use of a reflective reading can be used at this time each week as well. Encourage reflections and insights from the previous session.

Materials: Journal, Handout for session no. 4.

Exercise: This exercise focuses on allowing survivors to have "that conversation" they wished they could have had. Members are encouraged to read their letter aloud and reflect on their thoughts and feelings about what it was like writing those thoughts and feelings down.

Perhaps the most common thing survivors express is a feeling of not having closure regarding the loss.

The group discussion should focus on:

- What was the journaling experience like when given the opportunity for unfiltered self-expression?

- What insights did they gain about themselves?

As the members share and support each other through the process, they often see parallels in their experiences. As a result, this exercise generates sense of comfort for the participants knowing that they are walking "<u>through</u> the valley" with others.

There's comfort in knowing one is not alone in their struggle. Nothing is permanent, inclusive of intense pain from loss.

This is a good time for the facilitators to remind the group to reflect on the insights from the first exercise (Locogram).

This exercise also gives the member an opportunity to begin to think about their "tomorrow" by reflecting on what the lost love object would want them to be doing with their life in the here and now to move forward with love.

Upon the conclusion of the session, facilitators will hand out the session no. 5 journal writing exercise: Lessons in Forgiveness. **This is also a timed exercise, with the same instructions as session no. 4.**

> *"Sincere forgiveness isn't colored with expectations that the other person apologize or change. Love them and release them. Life feeds back truth to people in its own way and time"*
>
> S. Paddington

HANDOUT FOR SESSION NO. 5:

"Owning What's Yours and Leaving the Rest"

Lesson in Forgiveness

"An Open Letter of Forgiveness to my Lost Love Object"

Resentment and forgiveness are often unresolved when dealing with a loss. Prior to beginning journaling, here are a few things to contemplate as one meditates on how to "let go" and forgive?

- Recognition
Know what your feelings are regarding what happened
- Write down the details of the incident
- Identify what feelings come up as you write
- Sit with the feelings...experience them
- What was the action that wronged you?
- What was *your* part?
- What was *their* part?
- Be specific about what happened
Identify the "wrong"
- Reconciliation
- Making amends...with self...accepting from others
- Identify what you need and what you can do to move on...and let go!

"Forgiveness Is About You"
~ Katurah

OWNING YOURS

THE ZOLA EXPERIENCE

Introduction to Session no. 5
"Owning What's Yours and Leaving the Rest"
A Lesson in Forgiveness

Relationships are meant to grow us as human beings and to teach us life lessons along the way. The first and most intimate relationship is with one's family. Ideally, we are to learn life lessons at hoe that will help us become positive and productive members of this earth community as adults. One of the most important of these life lessons is that of "forgiveness".

Children seem to have a natural ability to forgive. They express how they feel. Their playmate validates their feeling and says, "I'm sorry". They both agree that everything is okay and they continue to play. With adults we tend to hold on to hurt feelings, sometimes FOREVER! Adults would have healthier relationships if they took the playbook of the children. Identify the feeling(s). Use the data, the information from the event, to validate their feelings. Finding and using their voice to express t*heir feelings.*

Perhaps the most important piece is a willingness to accept the outcome of making one's feelings known. There's generally one of two things that can happen.

Your feelings are validated by the other party and you are given an apology, or the other party remains stuck in THEIR old messages, and chooses not to recognize you and/or your feelings.

However things turn out, as Miguel Ruiz states in his book, The Four Agreements, don't take it personally.

You can feel positive that you expressed your thoughts and feelings. You can forgive the other person, recognizing they are who they are and where they are in their development, and forgiveness is really about "you". You can then choose to move lovingly forward with your life.

SESSION NO. 5:

"Owning What's Yours and Leaving the Rest"

Lesson in Forgiveness

At the beginning of the session, the facilitators check in with the group. The use of a reflective reading can be used at this time each week as well. Encourage reflections and insights from the previous session.

Materials: Journal; handout for session no. 5.

Exercise: The goal of this session is to foster self-insight regarding the loss and forgiveness of self and the lost love object.

Client's oftentimes struggle with "forgiveness". This struggle may center around the lost love object or of the self in relation to the loss. This journaling exercise gives them the opportunity to have a frank and open conversation and reflection with the "self".

Once there is awareness of "self-forgiveness", the person can then continue their journey of recovery from the loss. They have the opportunity to take ownership of their part and forgive themselves, and forgive that which is not theirs.

Studies show that Forgiveness:
- Decreases stress related health concerns
- Decreases Emotional eating
- Improves the energy level
- Good for the heart
- Lowers heart rate
- Lowers blood pressure

Upon the conclusion of the session, facilitators will hand out session no.6 journal writing exercise: Legacy Tribute. Participants will be instructed to design a tribute to the legacy of the lost love object. Continue to remind members to do "self-care".

HANDOUT FOR SESSION NO. 6:

"Letting go Through Creative Expression"

Legacy Tribute

Choose a tribute to the legacy of your lost love object.

What would you like to do as a remembrance to your lost love object?

It can be on a large scale, (i.e. an annual marathon; banquet; family community give back activity, etc.)

It can be on a small scale, (i.e. planting flowers; one-time book award; planting a tree; volunteering at a community event, etc.)

Be prepared to share your tribute at the next session.

THE ZOLA EXPERIENCE
A JOURNEY OF RECOVERY FROM LOSS

"The ZOLA Experience is All About The Healing Power of Love"

~ Katurah

A LEGACY TRIBUTE
Introduction to Session no. 6

THE ZOLA EXPERIENCE
Letting go Through Creative Expression

I have always admired artists and their creativity. A lot of artist talk about the love they have for their creations. It is the creativity that shows up on the blank canvas, or the new ball of clay. When one begins to think about what would be a fitting tribute for their lost love object, the sky is the limit.

Once one creates a Legacy Tribute, it allows them to continue to honor the loss from a place of letting go, a place of love.

"Letting go Through Creative Expression"
Legacy Tribute Choose a tribute to the legacy of your lost love object.

What would you like to do as a remembrance to your lost love object?

It can be on a large scale, (i.e. an annual marathon; banquet; family community give back activity, etc.)

It can be on a small scale, (i.e. planting flowers; one-time book award; planting a tree; volunteering at a community event, etc.)

Be prepared to share your tribute at the next session.

> **"Humor is healing's handmaiden."**
> Healing Runes, Humor

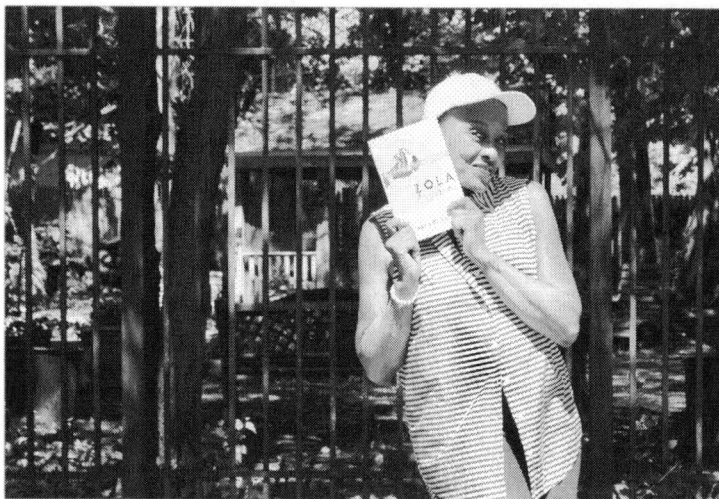

SESSION NO. 6:

"Letting go Through Creative Expression"
Legacy Tribute

At the beginning of the session, the facilitators check in with the group. The use of a reflective reading can be used at this time each week as well. Encourage reflections and insights from the previous session.

Materials: Journal; handout for session no. 6.

Exercise: This exercise is designed to allow creativity in the designing of a tribute to the lost love object.

The Legacy Tribute can be as simple as planting flowers or an annual 5K run to raise scholarship funds to recognize the legacy. Some have committed to volunteering for an organization as their legacy tribute. Members have been quite creative and generally are very supportive of each other to actualize their dreams.

The goal at this point is that the group has coalesced and gained a group identity. In the case of working with the individual, the client has gained insight, and has taken on a new identity in how they see themselves moving forward.

Upon the conclusion of the session, facilitators will hand out the final session no. 7 journal writing exercise: "Continuing Together as One".

The journal exercise for the final session:
- The members are to reflect on their ZOLA journey. Each member is to come with a name that reflects their group experience to share

- The individual can also be encouraged to do the same, to come with a name or phrase that reflects their ZOLA Experience

- If working with a group, the group can plan how they would like to experience the final session. This ranges from "pot-lucks"; presenting "awards"; it is a time of creativity and celebration of life and love

- The group is also free to share contact information at the next session

- Individuals can be encouraged to think of what they would like to do to honor this experience.

They can explore a wide range of ideas to celebrate their journey of life and love.

"Love is not bound by time nor frequency of contact, or physical presence. Love is infinite. Love is expansive. Love is forever."

Katurah Bryant

The ZOLA Experience

HANDOUT FOR SESSION NO. 7:

"Continuing Together as One"
"A Time for Reflection": The ZOLA Experience

Journal about your thoughts, feelings you have experienced and insights you have gained during the past six (6) sessions.

Be prepared to exchange contact information with your group members. Use a business card; 3x5 card with your address label and contact information; or give the facilitator permission to share your information with your fellow members that can be shared via email.

Begin thinking about a name to identify your experience over the past six (6) sessions.

"Understanding the remarkable metamorphosis of the butterfly, I also recognize recovery from loss is no less a miracle"
                    ~ Katurah

REFLECTIVE REVIEW

THE ZOLA EXPERIENCE
Introduction to Session no. 7

COMING TOGETHER AS ONE

I love groups. Wether I'm a part of one as a member or as a facilitator. They become a "family" as the foundation of a healthy system manifests in the context of the group interactions. Members begin to coalesce as they take risks to trust, talk and feel. In individual sessions the client:therapist relationship creates this dynamic as well.

The ZOLA Experience groups offers participants to come together to see the strengths they have as a group. The come to rely on the power of the group as a community. Reflecting on the journey from the first session to the last, helps to create a lasting bond, a true community.

It is truly a beautiful and remarkable thing to witness and be a part of.   As a facilitator it is truly an honor to serve and support this process.

The ZOLA Experience is all about the healing power of love.

"… and the greatest of these is Love"

SESSION no. 7

"A Time for Reflection"
The ZOLA Experience

At the beginning of the session, the facilitators check in with the group. The use of a reflective reading can be used at this time each week as well. Encourage reflections and insights from the previous session.

This is a session for reflection of insights and growths of the group/individual as a result of their ZOLA Experience. Members/individual reflect on the healing journey over the past six (6) sessions.

The group members share their suggestions for a group name/identity, and come up with a consensus. This gives the members a true sense of "community". They are now connected and identify with their support "family".

An identifying name is also done at the final individual session. This gives closure to the experience.

Members may choose to formally share contact information at this time.

The ideal goal is for the cohort to see themselves as yet another "circle of support" with members of a common experience of loss and healing from that loss.

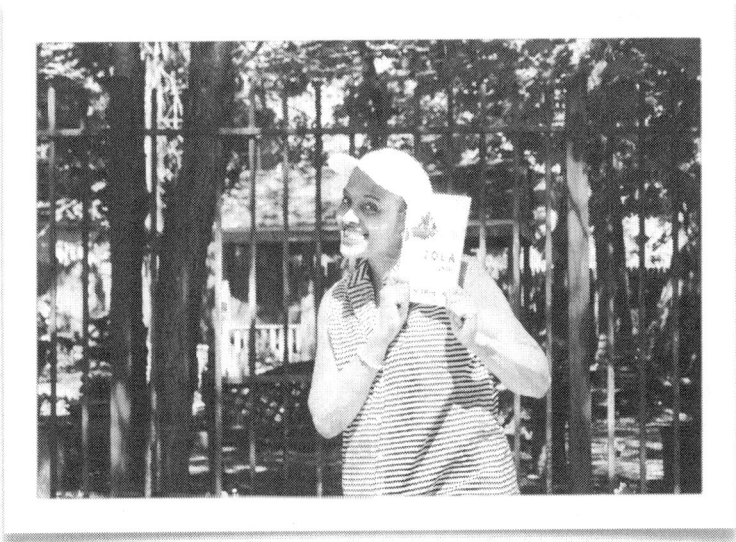

THE ZOLA EXPERIENCE
AN IMPACTFUL CERTIFICATION PROGRAM
FOR FACILITATORS

The ZOLA Experience is a certificate program for providers. Once you have completed the seven session as your consumers will, you will receive more in-depth insight regarding facilitating the sessions. You must have the manual " The ZOLA Experience:

A Journey of Recovery From Loss", available during this process of the training. Handouts needed for the facilitation of the sessions are contained in the manual, as well as journaling space. Upon completion of the training you will be given a certificate of completion of the training allowing you to use The ZOLA Experience intervention.

Why Facilitators Are Required to Complete The Zola Experience:

• Prior to beginning this journey with clients, facilitators are taken through the sessions. This is important so that the group facilitators will be aware of their own thoughts, feelings, and perhaps unfinished business of their own loss(es). This awareness will serve them to be able to support and guide the individual or members through their journey, with minimal contamination of the process.

Suggestions for Facilitators

- Weekly wrap up sessions for group facilitators are important as well. Not only to process the session, but to prepare for the next one.
- Evaluations by the participants for quality assurance. (see appendix)
- A final wrap up session is also recommended to review evaluations and for closure for the facilitators.

"THE ZOLA EXPERIENCE"
ADDING VALUE TO YOUR PRACTICE

This curriculum can be used in a variety of settings. The settings can vary from a formal treatment setting to a community setting. The curriculum can be used in an individual treatment setting as well.

In addition to working with clients that have experienced a death of a loved one, the curriculum can be used to address any loss. The process is similar across the spectrum of loss, separation, grief and recovery.

Facilitators must be mindful of cultural norms and rituals regarding loss in the community they are working with, and make the appropriate adjustments.

Groups can be gender specific; non-binary; recovery oriented. They can be composed of members with a similar challenge. For example, families that have experienced the loss of a child; a parent; a profession inclusive of "retirement"; a partner; a relationship; survivors of illness; body image changes to note a few.

The ZOLA Experience would be beneficial in the recovery process during the age of a "pandemic" when individuals are experiencing the sudden loss and the unorthodox transition with loved ones being in isolation vs supported by family during the transition. Other losses include but are not limited to: the loss of employment/income, housing insecurity, experience of social isolation as a result of quarantine, etc.

It is important to note again that grief and recovery is an individual experience. Small shifts of insight and "letting go" are major developments on the road of recovery from loss. An individual may go through the modules more than once in their quest to gain insight and to continue their recovery process.

"Wisdom teaches the mind to understand and learn through love"

Healing Runes, Wisdom

THE ZOLA EXPERIENCE
A JOURNEY OF RECOVERY FROM LOSS

CONTACT INFORMATION

Katurah A. Bryant, MS-LMFT, BSN-RN, LADC
Creator of "The ZOLA Experience: A Journey of
Recovery From Loss"

katurah@globalalchemygroup.com

CEO, Global Alchemy Group-Training Division
New Haven, Connecticut
katurah@Globalalchemygroup.com
www.Globalalchemygroup.com
203.915.6301

Please contact re:
The ZOLA Experience Supervision
The ZOLA Experience Trainer Certificate
The ZOLA Experience CEU's
Keynote and speaking engagements

> **"Don't ever discount the wonder of your tears.
> They can be healing waters and a stream of joy.
> Sometimes they can be the best words the heart
> can speak"**
>
> W. Young, The Shack

APPENDIX
ADDITIONAL HANDOUTS

- 18 Benefits of Deep Breathing
  - How to Breathe Properly

- Courage in Your Job Moment: Facing Challenges
- A Practice of Listening to Your Intuitive Voice

  - A Journaling Exercise: Listening to Your Intuitive Self

- Check List for a Healthy Relationship
  - The Checklist

- Affirmations
- Orientation Handout
- Sample evaluation
- References
- Bonus Journal
- Testimonials

THE ZOLA EXPERIENCE
A JOURNEY OF RECOVERY FROM LOSS

18 BENEFITS OF DEEP BREATHING

Anonymous. (n.d.). 18 Benefits to Deep Breathing. Retrieved from
>   https://www.onepowerfulword.com/ 2010/10/18-benefits-of-deep-breathing-and-how.html.

Breathing correctly is not only important for living longer but also to have a good mood and keep performing at your best. Let us look at the benefits of deep breathing and why you should make it part of your everyday living.

1. Breathing Detoxifies and Releases Toxins

Your body is designed to release 70% of its toxins through breathing. If you are not breathing effectively, you are not properly ridding your body of its toxins. i.e. other systems in your body must work overtime which could eventually lead to illness. When you exhale air from your body you release carbon dioxide that has been passed through from your bloodstream into your lungs. Carbon dioxide is a natural waste of your body's metabolism.

2. Breathing Releases Tension

Think how your body feels when you are tense, angry, scared or stressed. It constricts. Your muscles get tight and your breathing becomes shallow. When your breathing is shallow you are not getting the amount of oxygen that your body needs.

3. Breathing Relaxes the Mind/Body and Brings Clarity

Oxygenation of the brain reducing excessive anxiety levels. Paying attention to your breathing. Breathe slowly, deeply and purposefully into your body. Notice any places that are tight and breathe into them. As you relax your body, you may find that the breathing brings clarity and insights to you as well.

4. Breathing Relieves Emotional Problems

Breathing will help clear uneasy feelings out of your body

5. Breathing Relieves Pain

You may not realize its connection to how you think, feel and experience life. For example, what happens to your breathing when you anticipate pain? You probably hold your breath. Yet studies show that breathing into your pain helps ease it.

6. Breathing Massages Your Organs

The movements of the diaphragm during the deep breathing exercise massages the stomach, small intestine, liver and pancreas. The upper movement of the diaphragm also massages the heart. When you inhale air your diaphragm descends and your abdomen will expand. By this action you massage vital organs and improves circulation in them. Controlled breathing also strengthens and tones your abdominal muscles.

7. <u>Breathing Increases Muscle</u>

Breathing is the oxygenation process to all of the cells in your body. With the supply of oxygen to the brain this increases the muscles in your body.

8. <u>Breathing Strengthens the Immune System</u>

Oxygen travels through your bloodstream by attaching to hemoglobin in your red blood cells. This in turn then enriches your body to metabolize nutrients and vitamins.

9. <u>Breathing Improves Posture</u>

Good breathing techniques over a sustained period of time will encourage good posture. Bad body posture will result of incorrect breathing so this is such an important process by getting your posture right from early on you will see great benefits.

10. <u>Breathing Improves Quality of the Blood</u>

Deep breathing removes all the carbon-dioxide and increases oxygen in the blood and thus increases blood quality.

11. Breathing Increases Digestion and Assimilation of food

The digestive organs such as the stomach receive more oxygen, and hence operates more efficiently. The digestion is further enhanced by the fact that the food is oxygenated more.

12. Breathing Improves the Nervous System

The brain, spinal cord and nerves receive increased oxygenation and are more nourished. This improves the health of the whole body, since the nervous system communicates to all parts of the body.

13. Breathing Strengthen the Lungs

As you breathe deeply the lung become healthy and powerful, a good insurance against respiratory problems.

14. Proper Breathing makes the Heart Stronger.

Breathing exercises reduce the workload on the heart in two ways. Firstly, deep breathing leads to more efficient lungs, which means more oxygen, is brought into contact with blood sent to the lungs by the heart. So, the heart doesn't have to work as hard to deliver oxygen to the tissues. Secondly, deep breathing leads to a greater pressure differential in the lungs, which leads to an increase in the circulation, thus resting the heart a little.

15. <u>Proper Breathing assists in Weight Control.</u>

If you are overweight, the extra oxygen burns up the excess fat more efficiently. If you are underweight, the extra oxygen feeds the starving tissues and glands.

16. <u>Breathing Boosts Energy Levels and Improves Stamina</u>

17. <u>Breathing Improves Cellular Regeneration</u>

18. <u>Breathing Elevates Moods</u>
Breathing increase pleasure-inducing neuro-chemicals in the brain to elevate moods and combat physical pain

How to Breathe properly?

In order to breathe properly you need to breathe deeply into your abdomen not just your chest. Even in the old Greek and Roman times the doctors recommended deep breathing, the voluntary holding of air in the lungs, believing that this exercise cleansed the system of impurities and gave strength. This certainly is of great value to you in your work in the world. Breathing exercises should be deep, slow, rhythmic, and through the nose, not through the mouth.

The most important parts of deep breathing has to be regulating your breaths three to four seconds in, and three to four seconds out.

1. Inhale through your nose, expanding your belly, then fill your chest. Counting to 5.
2. Hold and Count to 3. Feel all your cells filled with golden, healing, balancing Sun light energy.
3. Exhale fully from slightly parted mouth and Feel all your cells releasing waste and emptying all old energy. Counting to 5.

Schedule your deep breathing exercise just as you would schedule important business appointments. Set aside a minimum of two 10 minute segments of time everyday although you can begin with two five minutes segments if you prefer.

Honoring yourself enough to schedule time with yourself is the first step in mastering stress. Tend your relationship with yourself and your relationship with life and with others will be enriched and deepened accordingly. Remember to share with your children and all your friends and loved ones so that they too can reap its untold benefits.

"The PAST is recollection, memory; the FUTURE is anticipation; the PRESENT is awareness...only the PRESENT is real and eternal"

D. Chopra

The Seven Spiritual Laws of Success

Courage in your "Job Moment"
Katurah A. Bryant, LMFT

katurah@globalalchemygroup.com

We have all experienced those moments in time when life seems too difficult, to much to bear.

Those times when it seems that God/the Universe/ our Higher Power has turned his or her back on you.

Perhaps you have lost your job, or you just walked away from your "SECURE job"(if there is such a thing in this day and time) to pursue your dream, the economy tanks out and what you thought you had no longer exists. The direction YOU planned to go in now seems so uncertain and directionless.

Your marriage/relationship is falling "apart.

Your "perfect children" aren't so perfect anymore.

You have more month than money to pay your bills.

And just when you thought it could not get any worse, life seems to have a way of reminding you that things can.

OR let's take it from another lens.

The time when you believed in your heart that you have been "divinely inspired" to be on this path, and the task seems insurmountable and you begin to think that God has really got jokes because you look around and say "No Way!" This is not humanly possible!

It is during these moments that I reflect on the situation that Job found himself in.

To familiarize ourselves with just who Job was, lets take a few minutes to describe this man.

Job was a rich man, one of the richest in the world at that time. He had a loving and devoted wife; 7 sons and 3 beautiful daughters. His family loved each other and regularly spent time with each other. And we all know that even in this day and time that is pretty awesome.

Job had many cattle, sheep, and acres and acres of land. He would be considered wealthy even in this day and time.

Job was also a very spiritual man. He gave thanks and praise to his God daily, and several times a day. **He** was so grateful to Almighty God for blessing him beyond measure. Job even made prayers of sacrifice for his family, just in case they might have done something to displease God during their day! Truly Job was "paying it forward".

We must understand that it was God that offered his servant Job to the fallen angel Satan, for his faith to be tested: "Have you considered my servant, Job".

Satan noted that Job was truly blessed by God and challenged God noting of course it is nothing to worship freely when you have everything including the protection of God. So God gave him free reign over Job. The only thing that could not be taken was Job's life itself, as God is the giver of life and death.

And then one day Job's world was turned upside down.

The first challenge: Job's oxen and donkeys were taken away by an unfriendly faction and killed all of the workers save one who brought the news of the destruction to Job.

WHILE HE WAS DELIVERING THAT MESSAGE….. ANOTEHR SERVANT came running to Job….he reported another challenge:

Fire from Heaven came down and burned up all his sheep and workers…except the one who brought the news of the destruction to Job.

WHILE THAT MESSAGE WAS BEING DELIVERED….ANOTHER SERVANT CAME RUNNING TO JOB…..HE REPORTED THAT

Yet another faction had taken Job's camels and killed more workers except the one that was delivering the message of the tragedy!

WHILE THAT MESSAGE WAS BEING DELIVERED....ANOTHER SERVANT CAME RUNNING TO JOB.....HE REPORTED THAT

Job's 7 sons and three daughters were eating and drinking wine in their eldest brother's house and great wind destroyed the house and his seven sons were killed.

Now in anyone's world this series of catastrophic traumatic losses would at best send someone into a catatonic state; not to mention questioning God as to what was going on!?

However…Brother Job…immediately connected with God and did prayers of worship and praise. He remained a man of integrity, a man of faith in spite of his recent tragedies…

Now if that was not enough God offered Job up again for the fallen angel Satan to challenge him yet again. Satan recognized that wordly possessions meant little. What would happen if he challenged Job's health, surely Job's response would be less perfect in the eyes of God

Job was stricken with sore boils from the palms of his feet to his head. Even his wife wanted him to give up his integrity as a God fearing and God loving man….

Job's response to her: " SHALL WE ACCEPT GOOD FROM GOD AND NOT TROUBLE?"

It was Job's courage in the face of adversity, and the ultimate challenge of his FAITH that brought him through. It took COURAGE for him to remain faithful and faith filled. His three friends heard about his adversity and came to offer their support and challenged Job to re-think his relationship with God.

Often our faith is "strong" when life is "good" and we think we got it going on! We got the job, the house, the 2.5 kids and money in the bank!

We believe we have the "courage" to do anything… go anywhere…and have limitless possibilities in life! Some even go to the extreme and become "boundary-less wonders" as evidenced by some in the "entertainment" industry; or the political arena, having lost sight of the needs of their fellow human being. Believing it is the worldly possessions that define them…that make them "highly favored"…

We have a smile on our face every day when things are going the way we think they should. We can at times begin to think that those who don't have it like we do are "lacking" something, that "they" are not doing something right. That "they" need only "pull themselves up by the boot straps" and they too will find favor.

What was it that allowed Job to get through what God had brought him to. And even more importantly, what did God KNOW TO BE TRUE about Job, that God would risk bringing him to such tests?

God knew this to be true about Job.

- ❖ He knew Job's character.

  - ○ After all, Job had frequent conversations with God, and his actions validated his words.

❖ He knew that Job had the courage to hold on to his faith and remain firmly planted in his belief in Almighty God, in spite of his "here and now" situation. Job knew that he could endure weeping through the night, because God had promised that his JOY would come in the morning!

❖ What God knows to be true about us is that our faith becomes stronger in the face of adversity and times of challenge.

❖ The Creator knows He is the source of our courage and strength to get us through, if we hold fast to God, just as Job did.

We are constantly given examples, that we sometimes call "miracles", of how someone became stronger and their spiritual connection became clearer after adversity.

Folks will say they don't know where they found the "COURAGE" to go on, if it were not for their spiritual connection, and God's grace.

Let's do a little journaling exercise:

- ❖ Take one minute to look at a snapshot of a moment in your own life

- ❖ Think of what might have been your greatest challenge?

- ❖ Reflect on the darkest moment of that event in your life. That moment when the light at the end of the tunnel was the size of the head of a pin.

- ❖ What were your thoughts at that moment that helped you get to the next moment?

- ❖ Who did you talk to? What did you do?

- ❖ What was your greatest source of strength that allowed you to persevere, that gave you the COURAGE to go on, to move toward the light, regardless of how small it appeared?

Now take a moment to reflect on that journey. What insights did you come away with?

I work with human beings challenged with Addiction and/or Mental Illness. I see these courageous people cross the threshold of our agency every day.

- ❖ Mustering the COURAGE to overcome their addiction and begin to establish a recovery oriented lifestyle, a healthier lifestyle.

- ❖ Having the COURAGE to deal with hostile systems that have lost sight of their humanness because those on the other side of the counter have lost sight of their own.

- ❖ Having the COURAGE to reconnect with a God, a faith, a belief that in the midst of their "JOB MOMENT" they believed their God had abandoned them, and then, coming to understand that their God is what protected them and gave them grace and allowed them to see "today", and their past as a place of forgiveness.

❖ Having the COURAGE to do their personal inventory to take an HONEST look at themselves and CHOOSE TO CHANGE.

The question is where do you stand in your "Job Moment"?

Will you have the COURAGE to hold fast to your faith?

Will you have the COURAGE to be the change that GOD WANTS YOU TO BE AND the world needs for you to be?

Yes, the WORLD! As it takes one "drop" to make an ocean, one step to walk a mile, one person to stand up to be the catalyst that CAN change the world...

Ask Harriett Tubman, before that first run on the underground railroad, holding fast to her vision of freedom from enslavement. Not just for herself, but for her brothers and sisters as well.

Ask Mother Theresa as she entered the slums to care for those who could not care for themselves, and choosing to live in the community she served.

Ask Rosa Parks as she refused to give up her seat on the bus. Her actions echoing the words of her ancestor and sister in the struggle, Phyllis Weatley, " Ain't I a woman'? Don't I deserve a seat on the bus to rest my tired feet?

Ask Martin Luther King, Jr... as he took on the leadership and raised their consciousness to force a nation to look at the most painful parts of itself.

Ask the multigenerational, multicultural supporters of Black Lives Matter, who are forcing us as a global society to see those from communities of color and alternative lifestyles as human beings and the historical impact of racism and other structural "isms" that don't allow people to be the best they were created to be.

 Yes, for all of them, there were challenges and obstacles to overcome. Some that seemed insurmountable, that only divine intervention could make happen!

What they have come to understand, and what all present here in The ZOLA Experience have come to embrace. If each one reaches one with an attitude and energy of love for our fellow human being, we will be the change.

The Creator/ Higher Power asks only two (2) things of us....

1. HONOR THE CREATOR/THE UNIVERSE WITH ALL YOUR HEART, MIND AND STRENGTH, with every FIBER OF YOUR BEING

2. LOVE your fellow human being as you love yourself **OR**

   want for your fellow human being what you want for yourself.

   If we do those TWO things, the rest of those 8 things on that

" Commandments" list will be taken care of.

Let us be like Job, by having the COURAGE to be faithful and faith filled in times of abundance, and most importantly in times of challenge.

And just as Job was, we will be rewarded and the world will be a better place for it!

Namaste….As-salaam Alaikum….Peace…Ashe' and Thank you!

Journaling as a Practice: Listening to Your Intuitive Voice

Katurah A. Bryant, LMFT

katurah@globalalchemygroup.com

We are all gifted with the guidance of our inner voice. Perhaps a more familiar reference might be "intuition", mother wit, or listening to your "gut". Whatever the reference, it is the Universe speaking to you. We often times do not pay attention to that intuitive voice, but most of us can recognize the guidance after the fact. You will hear people saying they should have followed their "first mind", or that they should have followed their "gut".

In the fast paced world we live in we must practice paying attention to hear that guiding voice within. Sitting still is the place to begin. When you have a decision to make, being still, taking some cleansing breaths, and being patient to hear, will position you to get in touch with the inner voice of guidance. Thoughts will come to you.

An excellent tool to bring you to an answer is to journal, where one is alone with their thoughts. Pen to paper is suggested. Allowing your thoughts and feelings to freely flow on to the paper brings clarity and direction. Keep writing until the answer comes. Trust me it will present itself. In my experience journaling for clarity, sometimes the answer would come quickly in a page or two. Then there were times when I would have written 10 pages of thoughts and feelings to come to the answer. Remember, practice makes it easier.

Here is a journaling exercise to practice getting in touch with your intuitive voice.

Remember, there is no "right" way to express yourself in your journal. This is a judgement free experience. There's no need to be concerned with spelling or grammar. Your feeling are uniquely yours, so just let it flow. Embrace the insight.

Happy journaling.

Peace, Katurah

A JOURNALING EXERCISE:

Listening to Your Intuitive Voice

Get comfortable and settle yourself with your journal and pen.

1. Think of a challenging circumstance or difficult decision you happen to be facing right NOW - Something that's been keeping you up at nigh

2. With this situation in mind: Write the first answer that comes up when you ask yourself the following questions … (Don't over think the answers. Don't think about the answers at ALL … JUST BLURT

   - WITH REGARD TO YOUR CHALLENGING/ DIFFICULT SITUATION:

     - WHAT WOULD BRING YOU A SENSE OF CALM ABOUT THIS SITUATION?

     - WHAT WOULD BRING YOU A SENSE OF PEACE ABOUT THIS SITUATION?

     - WHAT WOULD BRING YOU A SENSE OF RELAXATION/LETTING GO ABOUT THIS SITUATION?

   Given this insight…what are you going to choose to do today?

Check List for a Healthy Relationship....
Katurah A. Bryant, LMFT
katurah@globalachemygroup.com

Loving is defined in the dictionary as an adjective; feeling or **_showing_** love or great care. It is also identified as a noun: the **_demonstration_** of love or great care.

Both definitions denote "action". As I always say, "It's in the doing".

I was working with a woman who was struggling with finding herself in the context of relationships. She presented with a history of relationships that seemed to have a pattern to them.   All of which ended with her feeling discounted and emotionally bruised. In working with issues related to intimate partner relationships there are a number of things to consider.

Recognizing and understanding the impact of messages from one's family of origin are paramount. Your parents' relationship, whether present or not in your life, speak volumes to the child as to how couples are to interact. After all the parents are the first role models of relationships for the child.

How this plays out in the family system impacts future relationships. Children learn what they live, and adults live what they've learned. You learn how to communicate, what is acceptable behavior. You learn family traditions and rituals regarding births/parenting to deaths, celebrations to losses. It is when two people come together that all of these messages are challenged.

Everyone comes into the relationship with their idea of "normal". It's important for couples to have conversations to gain insight on whether they are on the same page, where they may differ, and if there's any room for compromise or does it come down to acceptance.

I began to think about something simple that one could relate to in an effort to support the desire to become more insightful in understanding a healthy relationship. The "Check List for a Healthy Relationship" evolved.

Recognizing that if there was a "no" to any one of the criteria, then one should give some serious thought as to whether the lack of that particular attribute would be a deal breaker.

Check List for a Healthy Relationship
Katurah A. Bryant, LMFT

As you reflect on the items on the list, the most important question to ask one's self is: "How *am I* like that?"

- Loving
    - God loving/spiritually grounded
    - Love of self
    - Loving behavior towards you
- Caring
    - Caring behavior towards you
    - Caring behavior towards others
- Trustworthy
    - " My word is my bond"
    - " My word is my bond"
- Compassionate
    - Has empathy for you
    - Has empathy for others
- Kind
    - Expressed in thoughtfulness
    - "It's the little things" ....random acts of kindness
- Considerate
    - Thinks of how one's behavior impacts others
- Generous
    - Generous with time
    - Generous with self
    - Generous spirit
- Honest
    - Honest in expression of thoughts and feelings
    - Truthful
- Integrity
    - Dependable
    - Ethical
    - Moral character
- Lives by the "Golden Rule": Do unto others as you would have others do unto you.

o   Respects the full circle of Karma; "What goes around comes around".

"To be aware of a single shortcoming within oneself is more useful than to be aware of a thousand in somebody else."

H.H. Tenzin Gyatso, the XIV Dalai Lama of Tibet

AFFIRMATIONS

You can either be a host to God/Higher Power...
or a hostage to your ego. Dr. Wayne Dyer

To know others is smart.
To know yourself is wise...
Anonymous

Trust the wisdom of the heart... Anonymous

When you are in tune with the unknown,
the known is peaceful. Anonymous
Every relationship we are in is a reflection
of the relationship we have with ourselves.
Akshara Noor

If I like myself, if I trust myself,
then the liking and the trusting will be
echoed in my relationship (with you).
Akshara Noor

A correct relationship to your self is primary,
for from it flow all possible right relationships
with others and with the Divine.
The Book of Runes, The Self

Use this day to simplify your life.
Bring harmony where you find dissonance
and balance where there is none.
Healing Runes, Innocence

Since self change is never coerced-
we are always free to resist-
remain mindful that the new life
is always greater than the old.
The Book of Runes, Strength

There is a place inside our being
where serenity dwells.
Take time each day to nourish yourself
with the comfort to be found there.
Healing Runes, Serenity

While you may be unable to change
your present situation,
what you can do is change your response
to that situation.
Healing Runes, Acceptance

I breathe out all pain and sorrow
I breathe in love and compassion
I breathe out all tension and fear
I breathe in peace and loving kindness
Book of Runes, Inner Peace

But, if it were I, I would appeal to
God/Higher Power; I would lay my cause
before Him. He performs wonders
that cannot be fathomed,
miracles that cannot be counted.
Job 5: 8-9

If you have but one wish,
let it be for an idea.
P. Sutton, Politician

Everything that IS was once imagined!
Ted Joans, Poet

Lose not courage, lose not faith, go forward.
M. Garvey, Nationalist Leader

Don't let ANYTHING stop you.
There will be times when you'll be
deeply disappointed, but you can't stop!
Sadie T. M. Alexander

Most of us love from our need to love,
not because we find someone deserving.
Nikki Giovanni, Poet

Be loving enough to absorb evil.
M. L. King, Jr

Love stretches your heart and makes
you big inside.
M. Walker, writer

The measure of a man/woman is
in the lives he/she's touched.
Erin Banks

Deal with yourself as an individual
worthy of respect and make every one
else deal with you the same way.
Nikki Giovanni, Poet

We are here to love each other,
serve each other, and uplift each other. Yogi

Where there is love,
there is no question. Yogi

I desire only that which God desires through me
F. S. Shinn, The Magic Path of Intuition

I desire the Divine ideas only to come to pass
under grace and in perfect ways
F. S. Shinn, The Magic Path of Intuition

I have an extremely hyper beneficial angelical
karma

For God has not given us the spirit of fear;
but of power and of love, and of a sound mind.
F.S. Shinn,The Magic Path of Intuition/2 Timothy
1:7

Do not let your heart's desire
become a heart's disease.
F. S. Shinn, The Magic Path of Intuition

Trust in God and the seemingly
impossible will come to pass.
F. S. Shinn, The Magic Path of Intuition

All unhappiness comes from not being
able to see clearly your good.
F. S. Shinn, The Magic Path of Intuition

Stand aside and LET GOD DO IT!
F. S. Shinn, The Magic Path of Intuition

I rejoice in my femaleness. I love being
a woman. I love my body!
L. Hay, Heal Your Body

I move forward in life with joy and with ease!
L. Hay, Heal Your Body

There is joyous release of the past.
Life is sweet and so am I. L. Hay, Heal Your Body

I am the power and authority in my life.
I am free to be me! L. Hay, Heal Your Body

I speak with gentleness and love.
I exhale only the good. L. Hay, Heal Your Body

I am a loving parent to myself.I am covered
with love and approval. It is safe for me to
show who I am. L. Hay ,Heal Your Body

I am perfectly happy to be me. I am good enough
just as I am. I love and approve of myself.
I am joy expressing and receiving.
L. Hay, Heal Your Body

I now choose to make my life light,
and easy, and joyful! L. Hay ,Heal Your Body
It is my Divine right to take my own
direction in life. I am safe. I am free.
L. Hay, Heal Your Body

I am at peace just where I am.
I accept my good, knowing that all

my needs and desires will be fulfilled.
L. Hay, Heal Your Body

I am free to ask for what I want.
It is safe to express myself.
I am at peace.
L. Hay, Heal Your Body

I love and approve of myself.
I recognize my own true worth.
I AM WONDERFUL!
L. Hay, Heal Your Body

I now choose to support myself
in loving and joyous ways!
L. Hay, Heal Your Body

Intimacy is that warm gift of feeling connected
to others, and enjoying our connection to them.
M. Beattie, The Language of Letting Go
Today, God, help me remember that during times
of transition, my faith and my self are being
strengthened.
M. Beattie, The Language of Letting Go

God, help me feel safe and secure enough today
to accept what I need to accept.
M. Beattie, The Language of Letting Go

The PAST is recollection, memory; the FUTURE is anticipation; the PRESENT is awareness. ...only the PRESENT is real and eternal.
D. Chopra, The Seven Spirituality Laws of Success

Think like a Queen. A Queen is not afraid to fail. Failure is another steppingstone to greatness.
O. Winfrey

Believe in yourself...for what you truly believe, you will achieve.
D. Latzke, When the Last ACORN is Found

Love others...and you will learn to give
Allow others to love you...
and you will learn to receive.
D. Latzke, When the Last ACORN is Found

Embrace your F.E.A.R:
Faith that
Erases old messages and fosters a positive
Attitude to allow you to
Receive! "The Gold Lady" aka Katurah

Good Things come to those who BELIEVE BETTER things come to those who are PATIENT and the BEST things come to those who DON'T GIVE UP!!!
Motivational Quotes

It wasn't a waste of time if
you learned something…
Motivational Quotes

To achieve something you have never achieved
before you must become someone you have
never been. Motivational Quotes

What you THINK is what you GET!!!
M. Taylor, The Daily OM

You don't have to know how LOVE
will manifest into your life, just prepare for its
arrival!…AND BELIEVE!!!
"The Gold Lady" aka Katurah

*"DON'T EVER DISCOUNT THE WONDER OF
YOUR TEARS. THEY CAN BE HEALING WATERS
AND A STREAM OF JOY. SOMETIMES
THEY CAN BE THE BEST WORDS THE HEART
CAN SPEAK"* W.Young, The Shack

Love is the language in which God speaks. and
when we listen with love, it is the heart that hears.
Healing Runes, Love

None of us can say with absolute certainty that one day will be followed by another. Nor can we say with certainty that one breath will be followed by another. Life is truly transient, and its transience is measured not from year to year, but from moment to moment. <u>The Tao</u>

EVERY TIME YOU FORGIVE, THE UNIVERSE CHANGES… <u>W. Young, The Shack</u>

Wisdom teaches the mind to understand and learn through love…. <u>Healing Runes, Wisdom</u>

Humor is healing's handmaiden.
<u>Healing Runes, Humor</u>

FIND YOUR VOICE AND EVEN IF YOUR VOICE SHAKES, JUST BREATHE… AND SPEAK YOUR TRUTH. <u>KATURAH</u>

CHILDREN LEARN WHAT THEY LIVE…
ADULTS LIVE WHAT THEY'VE LEARNED <u>Katurah</u>

MAY THIS DAY BRING YOU PEACE, TRANQUILITY AND HARMONY… <u>Yogi</u>

LIVE BY INTUITION AND CONSCIOUSNESS. Yogi

LOVE HAS NO FEAR AND NO VENGEANCE Yogi

LET YOUR HEART GUIDE YOU…. Yogi

LET YOUR HEART SPEAK TO OTHER'S
HEARTS…. Yogi

EVERYDAY IS A CELEBRATION AS WE
GET TO UN-WRAP THE GIFT OF…
"THE PRESENT"! STAY IN THE MOMENT…Katurah

WHEN IN DOUBT ASK YOURSELF…
"WHAT IS MY REALITY?"….. Katurah

GOD GRANT ME THE SERENITY… Serenity Prayer

The things we don't want to look at in ourselves
are the very things we need to look at. Daily OM

Be Impeccable With Your Word.
(Speak with integrity; use the power of your word
in the direction of TRUTH & Love)
M. Ruiz: The Four Agreements

Don't Take Anything Personally.
(Nothing others do is because of you)
M. Ruiz: The Four Agreements

Don't Make Assumptions.
(Find the courage to ask questions and to
 express what you really want)
M. Ruiz: The Four Agreements

Always Do Your Best
(Under any circumstances, simply do your best
and you will avoid self-judgement, self-abuse and
regret)   M. Ruiz: The Four Agreements

EXPECT A MIRACLE! KNOW IN YOUR HEART
THAT ALL THINGS ARE POSSIBLE. WE
COULDN'T CONCEIVE OF A MIRACLE IF NONE
HAD EVER HAPPENED. L. FUDIM

If you are having a "challenging" day...
YOU CAN CHOOSE TO START YOUR 24 HOURS
RIGHT NOW! KATURAH

"...AS YOU FORGIVE, YOU ARE FORGIVEN.
AS YOU LOVE, SO ARE YOU LOVED. AS YOU
RESENT, SO ARE YOU RESENTED. THIS IS LAW-
PHYSICAL, MENTAL AND SPIRITUAL!... LET THE LOVE OF
GOD SO FILL THY BODY, THAT THERE IS NO
RESENTMENT. E. CASEY (READING 2600-2)

Give "Time" time...and all things will change.
DeeBrown

Some of our disappointments are God
commissioned for us to change.
Pastor E. Morrison

God gave us two ears and one mouth that we
should lISTEN twice as much as we talk.
Ancient Proverb

Humor is healing's handmaiden.
Healing Runes, Humor

How I choose to respond to any challenge is
always up to me. This is my strength.
Relationship Runes

Wisdom teaches the mind to understand and
learn through love... Healing Runes, Wisdom

A Person's Actions Will Tell You Everything
You Need To Know. Unknown

People May Not Always Believe What You Say...
But They Will AlWAYS Believe What You Do
Unknown

It's In The "Doing…" <u>Katurah</u>

Trust creates peace…. <u>Yogi</u>

REPAIR…OR REPEAT! <u>KATURAH</u>

Love is the language in which God speaks.
and when we listen with love, it is the heart
that hears. <u>Healing runes, love</u>

HONORING AND ACCEPTING OUR PARTNERS/
SIGNIFICANT OTHERS, JUST AS THEY ARE, WITHOUT
NEEDING TO CHANG THEM, CAN BE A PROFOUND AND
HEALING ACT OF LOVE.
<u>HEALING RUNES, RELATIONSHIPS</u>

IT IS MUTUAL RESPECT THAT ENABLES ANY
MEANINGFUL RELATIONSHIP TO THRIVE
AND PROSPER. <u>HEALING RUNES, RELATIONSHIPS</u>

RESPECT IN ACTION IS DEMONSTRATED
BY THE CARE WE TAKE IN APPRECIATING WHAT IS
IMPORTANT TO THOSE WE LOVE.
<u>HEALING RUNES, RELATIONSHIPS</u>

THE COMMANDMENT TO "DO UNTO OTHERS AS
YOU WOULD HAVE OTHERS DO UNTO YOU" IS INDEED A
REVOLUTIONARY IDEA WHEN IT BECOMES A NATURAL
EXPRESSION OF WHO YOU ARE.
<u>HEALING RUNES, RELATIONSHIPS</u>

FOR WHERE THERE IS MUTUAL RESPECT-
REGARDLESS OF DIFFERING DESIRES,
OPINIONS, VALUES OR BELIEFS-LOVE WILL
PREVAIL. HEALING RUNES, RELATIONSHIPS

THE DIVINE IN ME RECOGNIZES AND BOWS
TO THE DIVINE IN YOU.
HEALING RUNES, RELATIONSHIPS

HONOR YOURSELF FOR YOUR COMMITMENT
TO THE HEALING JOURNEY. FOR IT IS A JOURNEY OF
SELF-ACCEPTANCE, SELF-LOVE, AND SELF-CARE, A
NOBLE JOURNEY OUT OF THE SHADOWS AND INTO THE
LIGHT. HEALING RUNES, SHAME

FIND YOUR VOICE AND SPEAK YOUR TRUTH. KATURAH

CHOOSING TO DO THE SAME BEHAVIOR WHILE
EXPECTING A DIFFERENT RESULT GOES AGAINST THE
FLOW OF UNIVERSAL LAW....ALL THINGS MUST
CHANGE. THE ANSWER IS IN THE SEASONS......
KATURAH

GOD/OUR HIGHER POWER GIVES US EXAMPLES
TO NOT FEAR CHANGE; THAT CHANGE IS
INEVITABLE. FIND YOUR BABY PICTURE!
KATURAH

You can't push the river ... Go with the flow.
DeeBrown

People today tend to take refuge in overwork
so they can avoid confronting their inner
turmoil. From be still and know , T N Hanh

Nothing ever ends without something else
beginning or begins without something else
ending.The little book of kitchen table wisdom R. Remen

Grieving is what enables you to go forward
 after a loss.IT HEALS YOU SO THAT YOU CAN
GIVE LOVE AGAIN.
THE LITTLE BOOK OF KITCHEN TABLE WISDOM

For, he that expects nothing shall not be
disappointed, but he that expects much--if he lives
and uses that in hand day by day--shall be full to
running over. E. Casey reading no. 557-3

Whoever gives to others will get richer;
those who help others will themselves be helped.
Proverbs 11:25

If you don't climb the mountain, you can't get the
view! Linda Rondeau from Soul Matters for Women

Life is busy and challenging, but some of the pressure we experience comes from our own unrealistic self-expectations.Soul Matters for Women

Even if others fail or desert us, our Higher Power (God) is always present in our lives.
Soul Matters for Women

The soul would have no rainbow had the eyes no tears.   J. Vance Cheney, from Soul Matters for WoMEN

Orientation Handout

ZOLA.....A JOURNEY OF LOVE...A JOURNEY OF LIFE

Welcome to the "ZOLA" Experience

Grieving from the loss of a loved one is as unique to the individual as one's fingerprints. No two people go through this process alike. The commonality of the experience of grief after a loss is that we all will experience it, and we all must find our way through the experience.

Recovering from the loss is a "process", not an event. When we think about our lives over the spectrum of time, we have been faced with loss and we have overcome the emotions that come with such an experience. As the elders would say, "Just live long enough".

We possess everything we need to get through the experience of loss and the life lessons that come with it. Sometimes one must dig deep to find understanding from a loss.

Then there are other times when the loss is clearly a mental and physical relief for the one who has transitioned as well as those that remain on this side of the plane. Regardless, the Universe makes no mistakes, and it becomes our job to understand the wisdom in the actions of one's Higher Power.

ZOLA is the essence of the process of grief; as well as the essence of life. Zola is an African origin word that means "to love". The moving on past the loss is a true testament of "Love"...love of self, as well as the transitioned loved one.

Over the next seven (7) sessions we will embark upon a journey to begin the healing process. Some of you present may be further along in your process of moving on than others. This will be a time of sharing with each other, not only about the experience of loosing a lost love object, but most importantly, of sharing what has helped you to move past the experience and embrace it as a part of life.

It is our hope that you will remain open to the process and allow yourself to take some risks to become more insightful, recognizing this is a new experience for everyone.

The seven (7) sessions will be facilitated by experienced facilitators/ clinicians to support you on your journey.

The group session will be one hour _____
You may arrive early to enjoy ask questions, so we may begin promptly.

You may be given simple tasks to complete between sessions.

It will be important that you allow yourself to be open to the group process. Remember, the goal of the group is to support each other through the process. Together... "Yes we can"!

We will touch upon several topics for discussion. Some of the sessions will be more experiential and we will have you moving.

Remember it's all about ZOLA...which means to Love....

THE ZOLA EXPERIENCE
A JOURNEY OF RECOVERY FROM LOSS

Session One: "Getting to know you"
Session Two: "We've come this far by Faith"...Spirituality in the face of grief
Session Three: Messages from Family of Origin: Family Rituals/Self Care: Traditional and non traditional avenues... "It's all okay"
Session Four: The Benefits of Closure
Session Five: Lessons in Forgiveness
Session Six: Legacy Tributes
Session Seven: Continuing Together as One

Your Group Facilitators are/ Contact information:

_____

_____

_____

THE ZOLA EXPERIENCE
A JOURNEY OF RECOVERY FROM LOSS

Sample Evaluation:

The ZOLA Experience.....A brief evaluation of your experience

Cohort : _____

Session/Facilitators:

Scale: 1. strongly agree   2. agree   3. neutral   4. disagree
5. Strongly disagree

1. The location of the sessions was conducive to the group setting: _____

2. The seven sessions allowed me to establish a foundation for my healing process: _____

3. The session I found most helpful in my process was:

_____

4. The session I found least helpful in my process was?

_____

5. I felt supported in my healing journey: _____

6. Name: _____/_____
    Name: _____/_____
    Name: _____/_____

7. I would recommend the ZOLA Experience to others:

_____

COMMENTS:

_____
_____
_____
_____

KATURAH A BRYANT
MS-LMFT, BSN-RN, LADC

Founder and Creator of "The ZOLA" Experience"

A Certificate Program For Providers

REFERENCES

Abdul-Salaam, Aquil I. Original Artwork by permission of the artist. 2020

Anonymous. (n.d.). 18 Benefits to Deep Breathing. Retrieved from
    https://www.onepowerfulword.com/2010/10/18-benefits-of-deep-breathing-and-how.html.

Beattie, M. (1990). *The Language of Letting Go: Daily Meditations for*
    Codependents. HarperCollins Publishers.

Brown, B. (2010). *The Gifts of Imperfection: Let Go of Who You Think*

    You're Supposed to Be and Embrace Who You Are. Hazelden.

Chopra, D. (1994). *The Seven Spiritual Laws of Success: A Practical Guide*
    to the Fulfillment of Your Dreams. Amber-Allen Publishing.

Garcia, A. & Sternberg, P. (2000). *Sociodrama: Who's in Your Shoes?*
    Praeger.

Garris, Lonnie, Jr. " Love is…" original poem by permission of the author.

Hay, L.L. (2002). *Heal Your Body: The Mental Causes for Physical Illness*
     and the Metaphysical Way to Overcome Them. Hay House, Inc.
     (Original work published 1976). Retrieved from www.hayhouse.com.

Hendricks, G. (1997). *Conscious Breathing: Breathwork for Health, Stress*
     Release and Personal Mastery. [Audio Cassette]. Audio Renaissance; Abridged edition.

Leech, Joe (2020) 10 Reasons Why Good Sleep is Important (Medically reviewed by Arnarson,Atli BSc, PhD) *Retrieved from www.healthline.com*

National Acupuncture Detoxification Association (NADA). 1985.
     www.acudetox.com

Ortner, N. *Instructions for TAPPING to manage stress and negative*
     thoughts. Retrieved from www.thetappingsolution.com.

Ruiz, D.M. (1999). *The Mastery of Love: Practical Guide to the Art of*
     Relationship. Amber-Allen Publishing.

Stanborough, R.J. (2020). *The Benefits of Listening to Music.* Retrieved
   from https://www.healthline.com/health/benefits-of-music.

Taylor, M. (2004). *Mindful Walking: Walking with Awareness.* Retrieved
   from www.dailyom.com.

YouTube: Tapp of the morning with Jake.

YouTube: Simple QiGong

YouTube: Binaural Beats

THE ZOLA EXPERIENCE
A JOURNEY OF RECOVERY FROM LOSS

"None of us can say with absolute certainty that one day will be followed by another. Nor can we say with certainty that one breath will be followed by another. Life is truly transient, and its transience is measured not from year to year, but from moment to moment."

The Tao

Bonus Journal.......

KATURAH A BRYANT
MS-LMFT, BSN-RN, LADC

Founder and Creator of "The ZOLA" Experience"

A Certification Program For Providers

THE ZOLA EXPERIENCE

A JOURNEY OF RECOVERY FROM LOSS

KATURAH A BRYANT
MS-LMFT, BSN-RN, LADC

Founder and Creator of "The ZOLA" Experience"

A Certificate Program For Providers

ABOUT THE AUTHOR

Katurah A. Bryant, is a published author and creator of The ZOLA Experience: A Journey of Recovery From Loss. Ms. Bryant has spent her career specializing in the field of Addiction , Mental Health and Recovery. She recently retired from the CT Department of Mental Health and Addictions Services, as an Assistant Director of the CT Mental Health Center-Substance Abuse Treatment Unit.

Katurah also brings a wealth of experience in integrative health as a Registered Trainer for the National Acupuncture Detoxification Association (NADA) where she currently serves on the Board as the Co-Chair of Training. Ms. Bryant has many years training health care and community providers in the areas of Cultural Competence and Inclusion, and the fundamentals of Counseling in the field of Addiction and Recovery.

Ms. Bryant served as an adjunct instructor at Southern Connecticut State University-Marriage Family Therapy program as well as at Gateway Community College-Drug and Alcohol Counseling program. Katurah is available for retreat facilitation, keynote speaker, Mistress of Ceremony and is also a voice over artist. Ms. Bryant enjoys journaling, dancing (swing-out and line dancing), nature walks and time with her family. Katurah is a native of Nashville, TN, currently residing in New Haven, CT.

Reflections of The ZOLA Experience
Testimonials

"I am Licensed Clinical Social Worker. I can heal myself. I turned down two invitations to join the group. I am a strong Afro-Latina woman. I can rely on God and myself! Wrong on all counts! The group allowed me the freedom to express my grief.

Do not short change yourself by missing out on an opportunity to be in an inviting and caring group of professionals and others grieving just like you. This is a necessary village. Healing is ours to claim. "
__M.E.Knight, LCSW, West Haven, CT__

"Losing a loved one is never easy. The feelings of loss often come with deep anguish and despair. The Zola Experience allowed us to move through the grief process of losing our mother without the heavy burden of these feelings. In that supportive and encouraging environment of Zola,
we strengthened our faith, renewed our peace, and left with a hopefulness that conquered
the heaviness of death. The Zola experience was invaluable."   __Dawn & Ann S., New Haven, CT__

"The things I learned far exceeded dealing with grief – we were learning how to deal with and navigate life. The Zola Experience was a God send for me and my family."
Bridgette R., New Haven, CT

I would recommend this to everyone because The Zola Experience helps with the healing process when you are grieving. I needed help and Zola rescued me and taught me how to deal with my new normal. I felt a tranquil peace after the Zola experience. Katurah, thanks for helping me through a difficult time in my life.
Jacqui T., New Haven, CT

A short time ago, I took part in a therapeutic model called "The ZOLA Experience". While I am skeptical about therapies and/or counseling in general, I found that the experience was refreshing and rehabilitative. With The Zola Experience, you are guided to understand that healing your mind and soul is a continual process. My journey isn't complete, but I am well on my way!
Holly T.

" It was a great experience. I wish it was longer" ; "Excellent !!"
Cohort: ZOLA Daughters Spring Forward"

"Very grateful for the experience. I am very grateful that you did not give up on us because the group was only three".
Cohort: "Comforting Common Friends"-2016

"Each session helped me to express my feelings. Everyone very supportive. I enjoyed interacting with others with similar experience. I looked forward to each session".

Cohort: "Over-comers" - 2016

KATURAH A BRYANT
MS-LMFT, BSN-RN, LADC

Founder and Creator of "The ZOLA" Experience"

A Certificate Program For Providers

Get a Limited Edition Autographed Copy of
The ZOLA Experience: A Journey of Recovery From Loss
Copy & Paste:
https://forms.gle/Re31LJdqdVvZbrMFA

KATURAH A BRYANT
MS-LMFT, BSN-RN, LADC
katurah@globalalchemygroup.com

Founder and Creator of The ZOLA Experience
A Certificate Program For Providers

Katurah A Bryant

a published author and creator of The ZOLA Experience: A Journey of Recovery From Loss. Ms. Bryant has spent her career specializing in the field of Addiction , Mental Health and Recovery. She recently retired from the CT Department of Mental Health and Addictions Services, as an Assistant Director of the CT Mental Health Center Substance Abuse Treatment Unit.

Katurah combines her wealth of nursing and integrative health experience as a Registered Trainer for the National Acupuncture Detoxification Association (NADA), where she currently serves on the Board as the Co-Chair of Training.

Ms. Bryant has many years training health care and community providers in the areas of Cultural Competence and Inclusion, and the fundamentals of Counseling in the field of Addiction and Recovery.

Ms. Bryant served as an adjunct instructor at Southern Connecticut State University-Marriage Family Therapy program and the Gateway Community College Drug and Alcohol Counseling program.

Katurah is available for retreat facilitation, keynote speaker, Mistress of Ceremony and is also a voice over artist. Ms. Bryant enjoys journaling, dancing (swing-out and line dancing), nature walks and time with her family. Katurah is a native of Nashville, TN who is currently residing in New Haven, CT.

CONTACT INFO:

203.915.6301
Katurah@globalalchemygroup.com

"THE ZOLA EXPERIENCE"

Katurah A Bryant

MS-LMFT, BSN-RN, LADC
Founder and Creator of
The ZOLA Experience
A Certificate Program for Providers

Avalable NOW!

THE ZOLA EXPERIENCE
BY KATURAH A BRYANT

2020

THE INAUGURAL & VIRTUAL
CERTIFICATE TRAINING FOR PROVIDERS

Fall & Winter - 2020.21

RSVP to Katurah A Bryant at
203.915.6301 or
Katurah@globalalchemygroup.com

The ZOLA Experience

By Katurah A Bryant,
MS-LMFT, BSN-RN, LADC
Founder and Creator of "The ZOLA" Experience"
A Certificate Program for Providers

Facilitated by: *Patrina S Reddick*

PIMOSH Publishing Company

P.O. BOX 7077 - Matthews, NC 28105
pimoshpublishing@gmail.com
203.617.8839